The Hens in Poultsville

J Pilgrim

Published by Terpstra Estate, 2024.

THE HENS IN POULTSVILLE

First edition. December 18, 2024.

ISBN: 979-8230027157

Written by J Pilgrim.

Also by J Pilgrim

The Trionian Saga

The Trionian Saga - Part One: Beyond the Border Mountains
The Trionian Saga - Part Two: The Hyna Sword
The Trionian Saga - Part Three: The Quest for Lyla

Standalone

The Hens in Poultsville
Sleeping with Crystal
Excel Your Wellness: Virtues and Vitamins
The Chi Key
Body Strengthening Strategy
Xcel Wellness Tai Chi

Watch for more at www.thetrioniansaga.weebly.com.

Table of Contents

The Hens in Poultsville - Have Fun Keeping Back Yard Poultry

The Hens in Poultsville will each introduce you to the fun topic of Keeping Backyard Poultry.

Hens are a great addition to the backyard as pets. In addition to being intelligent, friendly, and quirky, they are productive egg producers.

People enjoy watching the girls prance about the lawn, searching for bugs and worms. Hens have unique personalities and eccentricities that keep people entertained for hours.

Children can learn from hens about the natural world. You'll never get over the smile on a girl's face when she finds eggs in the nest box; or the cry of delight of a boy when he feeds hens with meal scraps.

Each hen of Poultsville will keep you abreast of the subject of having the ladies provide you with an eggs-traordinary supply of eggs.

Are you *egg*-cited?

The author was raised on a farm and kept poultry. As a teenager, he gave names to the hens and roosters and captured them in this long-awaited book.

This fun and informative book on backyard poultry keeping is a must for any young person who wants to spread their wings into this amazing hobby.

Now older, the author has retained his love for his feathered friends and shares advice for any chicken enthusiast.

Full of pictures, hen jokes, and play on words, this book is an easy read for the young adult who is interested in keeping backyard poultry.

So, without feather ado, chick it out right away.

Introduction by Rye

Kia Ora, he Rye taku ingoa, and I will introduce you to the fun topic of Keeping Back Yard Poultry.

Hello there! I'm here to introduce you to the charming, quirky, and surprisingly rewarding world of keeping backyard hens. So, without feather ado, let's get cracking!

Why Hens Make Great Pets

Hens aren't just farm animals; we're feathered bundles of joy that can bring life, fun, and even some unexpected wisdom into your backyard. Unlike most pets, we contribute to your household in multiple ways. Not only are we productive egg layers, but we're also intelligent, sociable, and endlessly entertaining.

Imagine us wandering across your lawn, clucking contentedly as we peck at bugs or playfully tussle with each other. Each of us has a unique personality—some hens are bold and adventurous, while others are shy and gentle. You might find one of us loves to perch on your shoulder, while another might prefer to stay on the ground, curiously inspecting your shoes.

We're also incredibly low-maintenance compared to other pets. No long walks in the park, no vet trips for vaccinations—just a little care and love, and we'll reward you with delicious, fresh eggs and plenty of laughs.

The Joy of Watching Hens in Action

My keeper, Johan, could spend hours just watching me and my flock sisters as we explore the yard. There's something deeply satisfying about our rhythm of life—scratching at the dirt, searching for tasty worms, and having animated "conversations" in our peculiar hen language.

We're natural comedians, too. Whether it's our funny waddles, the occasional clumsy misstep, or our unending curiosity about the world around us, we'll brighten your day in ways you didn't expect. The more time you spend with us, the more you'll notice how much personality and charm we bring to your backyard.

Settling into a New Home

When we first arrive at your home, we might feel a little nervous. It's a big change, after all! But don't worry—with a little patience and care, we'll quickly warm up to you.

Here are a few tips to make us feel at home:

- Spend time near us, speaking in a calm and reassuring tone.

- Offer us treats—fruits like watermelon and berries are a surefire way to our hearts!

- Make sure our coop is cozy, secure, and clean. A good first impression goes a long way.

- Once we feel safe, you'll see us start to approach you more often. Over time, you might even find us following you around the yard, eager for a little company and maybe a snack or two.

Spend Time Near Us, Speaking in a Calm and Reassuring Tone

When we first arrive, everything feels new and a little scary—new sights, new smells, and a new routine. One of the best ways to help us settle in is simply by being around us. Spend some time sitting near our coop and talk to us gently. Your calm voice will signal that we're safe and that you're a friend.

Avoid loud noises or sudden movements, as these can startle us.

Try using the same tone of voice each time you come near us; consistency builds trust.

Over time, you might notice us clucking back as if joining the conversation. These vocal exchanges are the first signs of trust!

Offer Us Treats—Fruits Like Watermelon and Berries Are a Surefire Way to Our Hearts

We love treats, and food is the quickest way to build a bond! Offering us small amounts of special goodies can help us associate you with positive experiences.

Watermelon: On warm days, nothing beats a cool slice of watermelon. We'll happily peck at the juicy flesh and seeds.

Berries: Blueberries, raspberries, and strawberries are among our favorites—like candy for hens!

Veggies: Small scraps of leafy greens, cucumber, or peas can also make tasty snacks.

Hold treats in your hand or toss them gently into the run. Over time, as we grow more confident, some of us might start taking treats directly from your hand. Just remember not to overdo it; treats should complement, not replace, our regular balanced feed.

Make Sure Our Coop Is Cozy, Secure, and Clean

First impressions matter! A well-prepared coop can do wonders to make us feel at ease.

Bedding: Use soft, clean materials like straw, pine shavings, or hay for our bedding. It should be cozy but not too dusty, as we're sensitive to strong odors or allergens.

Safety: Ensure the coop is predator-proof with sturdy latches and no gaps where unwanted visitors could slip in. At night, we prefer a secure, enclosed space to feel safe while we sleep.

Nest Boxes: Provide clean and well-padded nesting areas where we can lay our eggs. A little privacy makes laying time much more comfortable for us.

Ventilation: While the coop should protect us from harsh weather, good airflow is essential to prevent overheating or moisture buildup, which can lead to illness.

A clean, inviting coop not only keeps us happy but also makes your job easier by reducing the chances of disease or pests.

Once We Feel Safe, You'll See Us Start to Approach You More Often

Trust takes time, but it's worth the patience. At first, you might notice us watching you from a distance, hesitant but curious. As we start to feel secure in our new environment, we'll venture closer.

Be patient! Let us approach you at our own pace.

Avoid chasing or picking us up suddenly—it's better to let us get comfortable with your presence first.

Sit quietly nearby with some treats, and you'll soon find the boldest hens leading the way while the shyer ones follow.

Before you know it, we'll be following you around the yard like little shadows, hoping for snacks, attention, or simply to be part of your routine.

With consistent care and kindness, we'll not only feel at home but will also develop a strong bond with you. This connection is what makes keeping hens such a special and rewarding experience!

The Magic of Fresh Eggs

Ah, eggs—the golden treasures we gift to our keepers. There's nothing quite like finding a freshly laid egg nestled in the straw. Not only are our eggs fresher and tastier than store-bought ones, but they're also a reminder of the connection between nature and your kitchen.

The more comfortable and happy we are, the more eggs we'll produce. So, keep us well-fed, loved, and stress-free, and we'll keep your breakfast table stocked with the best omelets and sunny-side-ups you've ever tasted.

The Benefits of Kitchen Scraps

We hens are nature's recyclers! Kitchen scraps that might otherwise go to waste become gourmet snacks for us. Vegetable peelings, stale bread, leftover rice, and even fruit cores are some of our favorite treats.

But that's not all—we also contribute to your garden. By eating pests like caterpillars and beetles, we help protect your plants without harming them. Plus, our droppings are rich in nutrients, making excellent compost to keep your garden blooming.

We hens pride ourselves on being nature's ultimate recyclers! Those kitchen scraps that would normally end up in the bin or compost can transform into delicious snacks for us, reducing household waste and giving us a nutritional boost.

What Can We Eat?

We're not picky eaters, and our varied diet helps keep us happy and healthy. Here's a list of some of our favorite treats:

Vegetable Peelings: Carrot tops, zucchini ends, cabbage leaves, and broccoli stems are some of the veggie scraps we adore.

Fruit Cores and Peels: Apple cores, melon rinds, and even banana peels can make for tasty pecking.

Stale Bread and Grains: Day-old bread, leftover rice, or plain pasta are excellent energy sources for us.

Eggshells: If baked and crushed, eggshells provide calcium to help us produce strong, healthy eggshells in return!

However, there are a few things to avoid feeding us, like raw potato peels, avocado pits and skin, chocolate, and anything too salty or spoiled. A balanced diet of scraps alongside our regular feed keeps us in tip-top shape.

Pest Control Extraordinaire

Our benefits don't stop at recycling your kitchen scraps. We're also your garden's best friend when it comes to pest control. Let us roam safely in your yard, and we'll happily snack on harmful bugs, including:

- Caterpillars munching on your veggies

- Beetles ruining your flowers

- Slugs and Snails sliming their way across your garden

Not only do we protect your plants naturally, but we do it without the need for harsh chemicals, keeping your garden eco-friendly.

Turning Droppings into Gardening Gold

What we eat doesn't just disappear—it comes back as something even more valuable: our droppings! Rich in nitrogen, phosphorus, and potassium, our poop is a powerhouse of nutrients for your compost pile. When properly composted, it:

- Boosts the health of your soil

- Encourages robust plant growth

- Helps your garden bloom with minimal reliance on store-bought fertilizers

A win-win situation, wouldn't you say?

Reducing Your Waste and Your Carbon Footprint

By feeding us scraps and using our droppings in your compost, you're actively reducing the waste that goes to landfills and minimizing greenhouse gas emissions. Every banana peel and leftover slice of bread that we gobble up is one less item contributing to environmental damage.

A Sustainable Partnership

When you bring us into your backyard, you're not just gaining a source of fresh eggs—you're creating a sustainable system where waste is minimized, gardens flourish, and we live our best lives as your feathery friends.

So, next time you clean up after dinner, think twice before tossing those scraps away. Chances are, we'd love to turn them into something egg-straordinary!

Hens and Children: A Natural Bond

If you have children, we're especially great at creating magical moments. Kids love feeding us, collecting eggs, and watching us go about our day. Through these interactions, they learn where their food comes from and gain an appreciation for the natural world.

The sheer delight on a child's face when they find a warm egg in the nest box or see us eagerly gobbling up their food scraps is something to behold. We also help teach responsibility, as kids can get involved in our care by refilling water, scattering feed, or helping clean our coop.

Hens and children are a match made in backyard heaven! We have an uncanny way of enchanting little ones with our quirky personalities, friendly clucks, and the magic of producing fresh eggs.

Creating Magical Moments

From the moment your kids meet us, their curiosity is piqued. Our rhythmic clucking, playful struts, and eager pecking create endless opportunities for fun and fascination. Here are some ways we make backyard time extra special:

Feeding Time: Children love tossing us food scraps and watching us dart around in excitement. It's a simple act, but one that brings endless joy and laughter as we "race" to gobble up the tastiest morsels.

Egg Collecting Adventures: There's nothing quite like the wonder on a child's face when they discover a warm, freshly laid egg nestled in the coop. It's like finding treasure—and it sparks their imagination about how nature works.

Watching Us Play: Whether we're dust-bathing, chasing bugs, or simply exploring the yard, our antics provide endless entertainment for young minds.

A Hands-On Education in Nature

Caring for hens gives children a front-row seat to nature's wonders. Through us, they learn about life cycles, animal behavior, and where food comes from—concepts that are often abstract in today's digital world.

Understanding Food Sources: Collecting eggs from the nest box connects children directly to their food in a way grocery store trips never could. They see firsthand the effort and care that goes into every meal, fostering gratitude and awareness.

Discovering Ecosystems: As children watch us scratch the dirt for bugs or nibble on plants, they gain an understanding of how animals and gardens coexist. It's a simple yet profound way to teach the basics of ecology.

Teaching Responsibility

Hens aren't just pets; they're partners that encourage children to take on meaningful responsibilities. Even simple chores like feeding us or cleaning our coop teach kids valuable lessons about care and commitment.

Daily Feeding and Watering: Tasks like refilling our water and sprinkling feed into our run are easy for kids to handle. Plus, they give children a sense of accomplishment as they see how their efforts keep us happy and healthy.

Coop Maintenance: Older children can help clean our coop or collect old bedding for the compost pile. This task reinforces the idea that caring for animals requires consistent effort, but it also brings tangible rewards—like our freshly laid eggs!

Gentle Handling: Learning to approach us calmly and handle us gently helps children develop empathy and patience, essential qualities for building relationships with both animals and people.

Building Confidence and Compassion

Interacting with hens can have a surprisingly profound impact on a child's personal growth. Watching us respond to their care builds confidence, showing them they have the ability to make a positive difference in the world around them. Our affection—whether it's following them around the yard or pecking gently at their fingers—instills a sense of connection and compassion.

Unplugging and Connecting with the Outdoors

In a world dominated by screens and digital distractions, we offer kids a chance to unplug and immerse themselves in outdoor fun. Time spent with us becomes a welcome escape, a chance to laugh, learn, and enjoy fresh air while bonding with nature.

A Lifelong Impact

The lessons children learn from caring for us often stay with them for life. They develop an appreciation for sustainability, a respect for animals, and a curiosity about the natural world—all values that shape them into conscientious, compassionate adults.

In short, hens don't just make great backyard companions; we also make great teachers, friends, and sources of endless joy for children of all ages. We're more than pets—we're a source of magical, feathered memories waiting to be made!

Important Considerations Before Getting Hens

Before bringing us home, there are a few practical matters to address:

Local Regulations:

Check with your city council to learn the rules about keeping backyard hens. Most councils allow a small flock of hens but may prohibit roosters due to noise concerns. Typically, you'll be allowed up to six hens, which is plenty for a family's egg needs.

Neighbor Relations:

It's a good idea to let your neighbors know about your plans. Reassure them that we're quiet, low-maintenance, and odor-free with proper care. A promise of fresh eggs in exchange for food scraps can often turn potential skeptics into enthusiastic supporters!

Yard Security:

If you want to let us free-range occasionally, ensure your yard is fully fenced with high walls. We're surprisingly agile and might try to explore beyond the boundaries if we're not carefully contained. For extra safety, consider clipping the tips of our wings—a simple, painless process that keeps us grounded.

Keeping us Healthy and Happy is Simple:

- Provide a secure, weatherproof coop with fresh bedding.

- Make sure we always have access to clean water and quality feed.

- Spend time with us—we thrive on human interaction and love gentle handling.

In return, we'll give you far more than eggs. We'll bring laughter, life, and a touch of the countryside to your backyard.

Ready to Ruffle Some Feathers?

Summary

With a little love and care, we'll become your favorite backyard companions, brightening your days, and bringing a taste of nature to your life. So, are you ready to welcome us home?

Start your journey into the wonderful world of backyard poultry today!

Hens are a great idea to add as pets to the backyard. As well as being intelligent, friendly, and quirky, we are productive egg producers.

My keeper, Johan, gets a lot of enjoyment out of watching me and the girls prance about the lawn, searching for bugs and worms. We each have our own unique personalities and eccentricities to keep you entertained for hours.

When hens are first introduced to a new home, we tend to be a bit nervous, but with your reassurance we soon warm up and like to hang out with you. The more quality time you spend with us, *egging* us on, making us feel at home in your yard; the more we reward you with endearment and those oval white things...you know...*Eeggggs*.

Speaking on behalf of all feathery friends, we love children. Children can learn from us about the natural world and where eggs come from. I never get over the smile on a girl's face when she finds one of my eggs in the nest box; or the cry of delight of a boy when he feeds me with meal scraps.

Check with your local council on their rules for keeping backyard poultry. Some city councils allow up to six hens and no roosters, while other towns are more lenient.

You also want to keep your neighbors on board and let them know your plan before you get hens onsite. A promise of eggs for food scraps may win them over to your side.

Be aware too that if you plan to let the girls out occasionally to free-range, make sure your yard is fully fenced with high fences. You may need to ask an adult to clip our wing edges to stop us from flying over the fence to the neighbor's property.

In closing, we girls are easy to care for. With the right enclosure and protection from the elements; with your guardianship and with your kind handling, we will provide you with more than you give.

That's all from me, Rye.

About Hen Breeds by Bantam

Hello, Bantam here! I am going to walk you through some of the common breeds of hens which you can buy at the sales yard, at your local Poultry Farm, or online. So without *feather* ado, let us start right away. We come in all shapes and sizes from large Buff Orpingtons to tiny breeds like me - Bantam weight. And our egg sizes reflect our sizes too.

Choosing Your Feathered Friends: A Guide to Buying and Breeding

When it comes to starting your backyard poultry adventure, choosing the right hens is key. Not only will the breed you select affect the type of eggs you'll collect, but also the personality and temperament of your flock. Don't be shy about giving your prospective hens a thorough check-up before you bring them home. Healthy hens are a joy to raise, but sickly birds can cause stress and may infect the rest of your flock.

Here's what to look for:

Bright Eyes: A healthy hen's eyes should be clear, alert, and free of discharge. Dull or watery eyes can indicate illness.

Glossy Feathers: Feathers should be shiny, smooth, and well-kept, with no bald patches or signs of mites.

Shiny Comb: The comb—the fleshy crown on top of our heads—should be bright red and smooth. A pale or shrunken comb may signal poor health or malnutrition.

Planning for Space and Numbers

Before you rush out to buy your new feathered friends, take a good look at your available space. A happy hen needs at least 4 square feet of coop space per bird to move around comfortably. Overcrowding can lead to stress, feather pecking, and a drop in egg production.

Small Yards: If you're working with limited space, stick to three or four hens.

Spacious Yards: Larger areas can accommodate more hens, but remember that the coop size and run should grow proportionally.

Quiet Breeds for Urban Settings

In urban or suburban environments, choosing quieter breeds is especially important to keep the peace with your neighbors. While hens can get loud during egg-laying sessions (and who can blame us, really?), some breeds are naturally more subdued.

Here are a few top picks for urban settings:

Buff Orpingtons: Friendly, calm, and great with children, Buff Orpingtons are among the quietest breeds.

Brahmas: Known as the "gentle giants" of the chicken world, Brahmas are calm and docile.

Barred Rock: Hardy and reliable layers, Barred Rocks have a steady temperament and are relatively quiet.

Rhode Island Reds: These robust, dual-purpose birds are excellent layers and tend to keep to themselves.

What do you call an excited chicken? Hen-thusiastic!

That said, even the quietest hens can get vocal if they're unhappy, particularly when confined for too long. If we feel cooped up, you'll know about it! Be sure to let us out to forage occasionally so we can stretch our wings and scratch at the ground to our hearts' content.

Why did the chickens try to escape? They felt cooped up!

Egg Colors and Ear Lobes

Not all eggs are created equal—at least, not when it comes to color! One of the most delightful surprises of keeping hens is seeing the variety of egg colors they produce. Here's a quick guide:

White Ear Lobes = White Eggs: Breeds with white earlobes tend to lay white eggs.

Brown Eggs: Most other hens lay brown eggs, with shades ranging from light to deep brown.

Popular White Egg Layers

For those who prefer white eggs, consider these breeds:

Ancona: A charming, active breed that's known for its beauty and egg-laying ability.

Dorking: A heritage breed prized for its mild temperament and steady egg production.

Leghorn: Perhaps the most famous white egg layer, Leghorns produce medium to large eggs consistently. They are hardy and adapt well to most climates.

Sussex: A versatile, dual-purpose breed that's easy to care for and lays lovely white eggs.

Brown Egg Layers

If brown eggs are more your style, here are some excellent breeds to consider:

Black Orpington: A common choice in New Zealand, these hardy birds are large, dual-purpose hens that produce medium to large light brown eggs.

Plymouth Rocks: A classic breed known for its striped plumage, Plymouth Rocks are friendly and dependable brown egg layers.

Rhode Island Reds and New Hampshire Reds: These robust dual-purpose breeds excel at both egg production and meat quality, making them favorites for homesteads and backyard flocks alike.

Dual-Purpose Breeds: The Best of Both Worlds

Some breeds are considered dual-purpose, meaning they are suitable for both egg-laying and meat production. These birds are typically hardier and more versatile, making them a great choice for those looking to maximize the productivity of their flock. Popular dual-purpose breeds include:

- Rhode Island Reds

- New Hampshire Reds

- Sussex

Final Thoughts: Choosing Your Feathered Friends

The key to a happy flock is choosing hens that suit your lifestyle, space, and preferences. Whether you're looking for prolific egg layers, quiet companions, or colorful plumage, there's a breed out there for everyone.

So, take your time, do your research, and soon enough, your backyard will be filled with clucking, pecking, and the joy of fresh eggs. Happy hen hunting!

So, there you have it... choose your feathered friends! Bantam out!

About Coop Construction by Barb

Gidday! I am Barb! My part is to tell you about pet pen construction, known as a Coop.

Designing the Perfect Coop for Your Feathered Friends

A well-designed coop is essential to keep us hens safe, comfortable, and productive. Whether you're buying a ready-made coop or crafting your own, the structure should be functional, durable, and easy to maintain. Here's everything you need to know to create an egg-cellent home for your feathered friends.

Buy or Build: The Coop Basics

You can find pre-made coops at hardware retailers or garden stores, or you can build one yourself using online DIY plans. Either way, ensure your coop includes the following:

Protection: The coop should shield us from the elements and predators, including rain, wind, heat, and neighborhood cats.

Nest Boxes: Two to four dark, enclosed nest boxes (30cm x 30cm each) are essential for hens to lay eggs. One box per three hens is ideal to prevent squabbles.

Roosting Perches: Provide sturdy perches (20cm per hen) for us to roost at night. Elevated perches keep us safe and cozy.

A Chicken Run: A secure outdoor area lets us forage, peck, and stretch our legs while enjoying fresh air.

A Creative DIY Mobile Coop: Johan's Story

My keeper, Johan, got creative and built a fantastic Mobile Pet Pen using a large IBC (Intermediate Bulk Container). If you live in a temperate climate and want a mobile option, let me eggs-plain the process:

Preparing the IBC Frame:

- Johan separated the steel cage from the plastic container and removed the steel base.

- He bolted a sturdy wooden base to the cage, raising the structure slightly off the ground so we hens could enjoy access to the grass below.

- Clear netting was wrapped around the cage to keep us safe, while the base was lined with clear plastic sheeting for weather protection.

Creating a Roof:

- He made a slanted roof from clear plastic sheeting and secured it with wooden boards, allowing rainwater to flow off easily.

- Two handles were bolted to either end of the pen, making it easy to move to fresh grass.

Transforming the Plastic Container into a Hen House:

- The floor of the container was cut out, and a wooden base was added for stability.

- Openings were created to connect the house to the pen, giving us hens access to both run and house.

- For ventilation, Johan lifted the container's cap slightly using metal brackets and added an extra air hole at the back.

Adding the Comforts of Home:

- Johan installed roosting bars in both the house and the pen.

- He added two nest boxes and a dust-bath bin filled with loose dirt inside the house.

- This innovative setup allowed Johan to move our pen to fresh grass regularly and to place us in sheltered spots during bad weather. Maybe you can draw inspiration from his design to create your own custom coop!

Where to Place the Coop

Minimize Neighbor Issues: Position the coop away from fences or areas that might disturb your neighbors. Many local councils have specific rules about the distance required between hen houses and property lines, so be sure to check before setting up.

Secure Your Yard: Ensure we can't escape into the neighbor's property. After all, you don't want to hear the classic joke—Why did the chicken cross the road?—because of us!

Weatherproofing and Ventilation

Since our house will be exposed to the elements year-round, make sure it's:

Weatherproof: Rain and wind should stay out, while the interior remains dry and cozy.

Well-Ventilated: Proper airflow keeps the coop fresh and prevents respiratory issues, but avoid drafts, as they can make us sick.

Nest Box Tips:

Place nest boxes in dark, quiet corners of the coop where we feel safe and private. Loud noises or constant disturbances (like children peeking in too often) can stress us out and temporarily stop us from laying. Check the nest boxes only once a day.

Cleaning and Maintenance

Keeping the coop clean is crucial for our health. Commercial coops often have sliding floors or removable trays for easy cleaning, but if you're building your own, ensure all areas are accessible for scrubbing and disinfecting.

The Mobile Coop Advantage

A mobile coop is an excellent option if you have a lawn. As we forage, we tend to scratch and peck at the ground, leaving bare patches in our wake. With a mobile pen:

- You can rotate our grazing areas to protect your lawn.

- You can move the pen to shaded or sheltered spots during extreme weather.

- We get access to fresh bugs and grass while your yard stays intact.

- Mobile coops often have wheels or sliders to make relocation easy. This design is especially helpful for smaller yards or urban spaces.

Perches and Roosting Bars

Roosting is a natural behavior for us hens. We feel safest sleeping off the ground, so make sure our perches are:

- 800cm Off the Ground: Elevation keeps us comfortable and away from ground-dwelling pests.

- 1.5-2cm in Diameter: Rounded edges help protect our delicate feet.

- Sturdy and Spacious: Allow 20cm of perch space per hen to ensure everyone has room to roost.

For variety, you can include multiple roosting levels inside the coop. Johan even added an outdoor perch in the run so we could enjoy the sunshine while keeping an eye on the yard.

Space Requirements

Each hen needs a minimum of 2 square feet (43cm x 43cm) inside the coop. Overcrowding can lead to aggressive behavior like feather pecking, which can escalate into serious injuries. Happy hens are hens with enough personal space!

Final Thoughts: Creating an Egg-cellent Hen House

Whether you go for a stationary coop, a mobile pen, or a hybrid design like Johan's, the key is to prioritize our comfort, safety, and well-being.

A thoughtful, well-constructed coop makes us happier and healthier, which means more eggs and more enjoyment for you.

So, a coop can be bought from various hardware retailers or constructed at home following an online DIY plan. The coop should include a house, providing protection from the elements; two to four dark nest boxes (30cmx30cm); perches for roosting (20cm span for each hen); and a chicken run where the girls can enjoy foraging in the fresh air.

Set up the coop in a place that is least likely to cause a nuisance to neighbors. Check with your local council rules to see the distance the hen house must be from the neighbor's fence line. It is important that we girls are confined to your property and can't visit the neighbor's yard. Do not let the hen cross the road... we all know how that turns out: everyone thinks it's a joke!

As our house is going to be outside in the elements, make sure the coop is weatherproof and the nesting boxes are kept dry. Ventilation is good; draft is bad for us. One nest box per three hens is ideal. The nest boxes need to be in a darkened area away from sunlight. Privacy is crucial for us to feel safe to lay you a *golden egg*. Any loud noise or continual disturbance can temporarily put us off laying. Parents need to make sure their children don't check the nest boxes more than once a day.

A coop positioned on grass will mean that after a few days, we girls will have scratched away at it while looking for bugs: so, it is unlikely that your lawn will remain pristine for very long. The remedy is to have a mobile pen or allow us out to forage on occasion.

Mobile coops generally have wheels or sliders, so that you simply move the hen house around to let the hens forage in different spaces - also good for placing the pen in a protected spot during extreme weather events.

Hen houses should be kept clean and draught free with perches/roosts a minimum of 800cm off the ground. The wooden perches should be 1.5 to 2cm in diameter with edges rounded, to protect our pretty feet. The perches/roosts should be long enough to accommodate all the flock (20cm space for each hen) and be positioned inside the house.

Regarding hen house space, there should be a minimum of 2 square feet (43cm x 43cm) per bird. If we don't have enough room, we can pick on each other and peck each other, drawing blood. You know the saying, 'united we stand; divided we *fowl*.'

So, there you have it from me, Barb. I hope I have helped you on your way to housing your feathered friends in an *egg*-cellent way. I'm off to a *hen* party. Sister's rule!

About Feed and Water by Paspalum

Why wasn't the chicken interested in going to KFC?

It wasn't on her bucket list.

Hey! Paspalum here. I've been asked to talk to you about what to feed your girls.

Feeding and Watering Your Hens: A Guide to Happy, Healthy Chickens

Keeping us hens well-fed and hydrated is essential for our health, happiness, and egg production. With a few simple practices, you can ensure we thrive and reward you with delicious eggs. Here's an in-depth look at our dietary needs and some tips for keeping us in clucking-good shape!

Check Feed and Water Twice Daily

Regularly monitoring our food and water supplies is the cornerstone of good care. Refill containers in the morning and evening to ensure we always have access to fresh, clean essentials.

Layer Feed: Commercial hen pellets or mash mixes are ideal as they're formulated to include the balanced vitamins and minerals we need for egg-laying and overall health.

Veggie Scraps: Supplementing our feed with vegetable scraps adds variety and keeps us entertained while we peck and forage.

Tip for Cold Weather: On chilly days, mix layer mash with warm water to provide warmth and comfort to our crops. This little extra effort goes a long way in helping us stay cozy during colder months.

Daily Feed Quantities and Preferences

Each of us will consume about 100g–150g (3½oz–5¼oz) of feed per day, depending on the season and our activity levels. Beyond our standard feed, we have some favorite snacks:

Seeds, Apple Chunks, and Greens: These are our go-to treats and are great for snacking.

Corn Cobs and Grapes: Fun to peck at and easy to digest.

Watermelon and Porridge: Perfect hydrating or hearty options, especially in summer or winter.

Dinner Leftovers: We're omnivores and can eat most things you do, but be careful about certain foods (see below).

Foods to Avoid

While we'll happily peck at most foods, some kitchen scraps can be harmful or even toxic:

Green Potato Peels: Contain solanine, which is poisonous to us.

Onion Skins and Orange Peels: These are tough for us to digest.

Dried Beans: Contain hemagglutinin, a compound that can harm us.

Avocado (Pits and Skin): Contains persin, which is toxic to birds.

Limit Sugary Foods: While corn and fruit are tasty, too much sugar can upset our digestion, so offer these treats in moderation.

Invest in Hanging Feed and Water Dispensers

Hanging containers are a game-changer for keeping feed and water clean and accessible:

Optimal Height: Hang the containers at our head height so we can easily reach them without spilling or walking through them.

Cool Water: Place water dispensers in the shade to keep the water cool and free from algae or contaminants.

Rodent Protection: Hanging containers also help prevent scavengers, like rats and mice, from accessing our food.

Water Needs: Each of us drinks 500ml to 900ml of water daily, depending on the weather. On hot days, we'll drink even more, so check our water supply often. If skillful, engineer an automated water supply to the trough.

Health Tip: Add a weak solution of apple cider vinegar to our water occasionally. It promotes digestion, boosts our immune system, and helps maintain overall health.

Grit and Calcium: Essential for Digestive Health and Eggshell Quality. Unlike humans, we hens don't have teeth, so we rely on grit to help break down our food in the gizzard. Calcium, on the other hand, is critical for producing strong eggshells. Here's how to keep us supplied with both:

Grit: Free-range hens can find grit naturally by foraging, but if we're confined to a run, provide alternatives like river sand or crushed granite.

Calcium Sources: Mashed oyster shell is an excellent calcium supplement. Recycled eggshells can also work! Dry them in the oven and crush them into small pieces before scattering them in our run. Just don't give us raw, whole eggshells, or we might develop a taste for eating our own eggs.

Kelp products or even leftover fish n' chips (in moderation) can provide a boost of salt and trace minerals.

Food and Egg Quality

What we eat directly impacts the quality of our eggs. Want deep yellow yolks that taste amazing? Incorporate these into our diet:

Dark Leafy Greens: Spinach, kale, or Swiss chard.

Wheat Grass and Alfalfa Sprouts: These are excellent for vibrant yolks.

High-Quality Feed: Balanced commercial feed ensures steady egg production and strong shells.

Preventing Pecking Disorders with Food

Pecking disorders often arise when we're bored or feel crowded. Enrichment activities, variety in diet, and plenty of space can keep us occupied and content. A few ideas:

- Scatter seeds or grains in the run to encourage natural foraging.

- Hang leafy greens or vegetables in the pen to give us something fun to peck at.

- Rotate treat types to keep things exciting and stimulate our curiosity.

Container Placement and Maintenance

Keep grit, calcium, and feed containers stable and sanitary:

Ensure containers are placed where we can't tip them over or step into them.

Hanging containers are ideal—they're easier to top up and keep everything tidy.

Efficiency Tip: Use containers large enough to hold a day or two's supply of feed and water, so you don't need to refill them constantly.

Final Summarizing Thoughts: Keep Us Happy and Full!

Feeding and hydrating your hens is one of the easiest and most rewarding parts of chicken-keeping. By providing us with the right nutrition, clean water, and occasional treats, you'll keep us healthy, entertained, and laying eggs like champions.

Layer hens need commercial hen pellets or mash mix, as well as vegetable scraps. It is a good idea during colder days to mix layer mash with warm water to provide warmth to the girl's crops.

Commercial layer feed contains a balanced mix of vitamins and minerals, pullets need to produce eggs and stay healthy. On average, each hen will consume between 100g – 150g (3½oz – 5¼oz) per day throughout the year. We girls will go nuts over seeds, apple chunks, greens, corn cobs, grapes, watermelon, porridge, and leftovers from your dinner.

Be aware that certain kitchen scraps can be toxic to chickens, such as green potato peels, orange peels, onion skin, dried beans, or avocados.

Give us plenty of leafy greens and limit rich sugary foods, such as corn and fruit. Chickens are omnivores and will eat anything people do.

Invest in hanging feed and water dispensers. Make sure that the hangers are bird-height because it makes it easier to partake from. Also, make sure the water is hung in the shade, so it is kept cool and free from contaminants. Hanging containers will also keep the contents from becoming soiled and give protection from scavenging rodents.

We girls each drink between 500ml to 900ml of water per day - depending on the weather conditions. Hey, here is a good tip to keep us ladies healthy: occasionally, dilute a weak solution of apple cider vinegar into the drinking water.

Full-grown chickens need a daily supply of chicken feed, grit, and water. Keeping us happy is easy when we have plenty to eat and drink. Hens only tend to fall into pecking disorders when they're bored, and food is the perfect way to keep your girls occupied.

Hens require grit. Remember we don't have teeth to break up food in the gullet. You have heard the saying, 'as scarce as hen's teeth.' This is another benefit of allowing us to free-range: so, we can find grit for ourselves.

Egg shells are around ninety-four percent calcium. A *little bird* told me that you can recycle these empty shells back into our diet. Probably, once a month, take dry empty eggshells, crush them up, and scatter them in your hens' run. This will recycle grit as well as give us something to forage for. Do not give us raw whole eggshells, or we'll get a fancy and start eating our own eggs.

What your hens eat not only affects the quality of the eggs but also their color. For deep yellow yolks, give them dark leafy green veggies, wheat grass, or alfalfa sprouts.

Just one more thing on the subject: hanging containers can be topped up with pellets and water so you do not have to continually refill them... easy aye? All this talk of food is making me hungrryy... Paspalum signing out!

About Egg Production by Clover

What's up? My name is Clover, and I am going to keep you a*breast* of the subject of having the ladies provide you with an *eggs*-traordinary supply of eggs. Are you *egg*-cited?

Egg Production: All You Need to Know

We hens are incredible creatures, working tirelessly to gift you with fresh, delicious eggs. But understanding the nuances of our egg-laying cycles can help you become an even better keeper. Here's everything you need to know about our production patterns, the factors that influence them, and tips for maintaining a happy, productive flock.

When Do Hens Start Laying Eggs?

We hens begin laying when we're about six months old, entering the teenage stage of our lives—this is when we're called pullets. At this age, we're eager and energetic, and if properly cared for, we can lay productively for up to three years. However, egg production tends to decline after this period as we gracefully age into retirement.

The Role of Light in Egg-Laying

Daylight hours are critical to our internal rhythms and egg production. Our bodies respond to light exposure, and longer daylight hours stimulate us to lay eggs. In spring and summer, when the days are long, we work diligently "around the cluck." But come autumn and winter, with fewer daylight hours, we tend to slow down production.

Why the Slowdown?

It's our natural cycle to take a winter break to conserve energy and focus on maintaining our health.

A lack of light signals our bodies to halt egg production temporarily.

Commercial Farming Practices:

In commercial egg production, farmers often extend artificial lighting in hen sheds to mimic long daylight hours. This tricks hens into laying consistently year-round. While effective, it's not ideal for backyard flocks, as it doesn't align with our natural cycles. Instead, embrace our seasonal break—it helps us recharge for the prolific months ahead.

Setting Up Nest Boxes for Happy Laying

Nest boxes are our private sanctuaries, where we like to do our egg-laying business. To keep us comfortable and productive:

Bedding: Line the boxes with newspaper at the base to prevent rising damp, topped with hay or straw to create a soft, cozy nest.

Privacy: Nest boxes should exclude direct sunlight and be positioned in quiet areas. We need peace to feel safe and comfortable enough to lay.

Maintenance: Check the bedding weekly. Replace it if it's soiled or damp. If you find a broken egg, clean the area thoroughly and add fresh bedding.

Tip: We naturally create a crater in the bedding to hold our eggs, so don't worry if we rearrange the straw—it's just part of our nesting process!

Why did the hen show off her eggs?

To set a good *egg*-xample!

Why Do Hens Stop Laying?

There are several reasons why we may take a break from egg production:

Moulting Season: Once a year, usually in late autumn, we shed our old feathers and grow new ones. This process, called moulting, requires a lot of energy, so we temporarily pause egg production.

During this time, you might notice our combs and wattles looking duller than usual.

Relax—by spring, we'll be back with renewed energy and plenty of oval beauties to meet your egg-spectations!

Diet Imbalances: If our diet is too low in protein or overloaded with sugary treats, it can affect our ability to lay. We need balanced nutrition to maintain the muscle tone and health required for consistent egg-laying.

Broodiness: Sometimes, one of us might become "clucky" or broody, meaning we're intent on hatching eggs—even if they're not fertilized! During this phase, we'll remain in the nest box, refusing to budge.

To break a broody hen, remove her from the nest box, offer food and water, and disrupt the nesting setup by removing bedding material.

Alternatively, let her ride out her maternal instincts. Ensure she has access to food and water nearby, as her body temperature will be high during this phase.

Tip: Collect eggs daily to discourage broodiness and keep us focused on laying.

Stress or Environmental Changes: We're creatures of habit, and sudden changes can stress us out, affecting egg production.

Moving the coop, predators prowling nearby, or overenthusiastic toddlers chasing us can all cause disruptions.

Provide a calm, consistent environment with a regular routine to help us feel secure.

Social Dynamics and Egg-Laying: We hens live within a defined pecking order, with an alpha hen ruling the roost. While this hierarchy is natural, excessive bullying can stress the lower-ranking hens, reducing their egg-laying capacity.

To limit aggression, ensure the coop is spacious, with plenty of perches and nest boxes.

Allow us to free-range during the day to reduce territorial disputes.

Summarizing Maintenance Tips

As our keeper, your care directly impacts our productivity. By understanding our natural cycles and providing balanced nutrition, a clean environment, and a stress-free routine, you'll help us lay consistently and happily.

Light, especially daylight hours are key to a hen's rhythmic *cluck*. When the daylight hours are long, we hens work around the *cluck;* but when colder, darker seasons come, we girls start to cry *fowl* and lay fewer eggs.

A Commercial farming technique is to apply light in the sheds for extended hours to trick the hens into producing, working the sisters 'from nine to five.'

Don't be confused though, the backyard nest boxes must exclude sunlight and be private for us to do our business. It is part of our natural cycle to allow the girls a winter break.

In the nest boxes, lay down newspaper and on top of this, hay or straw is traditionally used to make a soft bed. The newspaper will stop rising damp and aid in the quick clean-up of the nest. The hen will ruff the straw into a crater, in which to drop her parcel. You, as the keeper, must check the nesting material weekly and replace it if it is soiled. It is rare, but if you find a broken egg in the nest, clean it up and add more bedding material.

Here are some of the reasons why we ladies take a break:

Once a year, usually, in late autumn, hens moult – meaning we shed some feathers. During this season, we chooks aren't able to produce the same number of eggs, because we are regrowing plumage. You will also notice our combs and wattles are duller than usual, giving you a sign that we are off-lay.

Relax, cause in the spring, we will be back with fervor and meet all your *egg*-spectations.

At other times of the year, if a hen goes off-lay, maybe their diet is lacking in protein and too rich in sugary treats. Keep us girls looking like athletes, full of muscle, not flab.

Sometimes, a hen becomes set on hatching her eggs, even if they are not fertilized, and will remain in the nest box. This is called 'broody' or 'going clucky.' You won't be able to move her off the eggs unless by force. Some breeds are more prone to 'going clucky' than others: Rhode Island Reds and Bantams for instance.

What do confused chickens lay?

Scrambled eggs.

Stress can also affect your laying ladies. Any sudden movements can put the yellow streak up us, like moving the coop without paying attention to our safety or getting a fright from a predator or an overenthusiastic toddler. Ensure we have a regular routine and are treated with res*peck*t.

Chickens operate in a highly defined social structure. There's an alpha hen in every flock, and hens will peck at each other to establish who's boss. You have heard of the sayings, 'pecking order' and 'hen-pecked.' If hens at the bottom of the order are picked on too much by the top hens, then this can also mean that egg-laying will not be all it has *cracked* up to be. Although this is a natural behavior, you can limit the bullying by making sure your coop is spacious and that we free-range during the day.

So, all chicken keepers out there, I know that you want to do an egg-cellent job when caring for your feathered friends: make sure that you've got the knowledge you need to raise a happy, healthy flock.

Before I sign off, let me leave you with one last thought: What's a hen's favorite subject to study? Egg-onomics!

Now go out there and cluck with confidence, knowing you're equipped to raise a healthy, happy flock! Clover Out!

About Common Pests by Thistle

Hello there. Thistle is my name and cleanliness is the name of my game! I am going to talk about pests that can worry your girls and how you can keep a*breast* of the situation.

Pest Control in the Backyard Flock

Let's talk about managing pests in your backyard flock. These pesky invaders can cause discomfort and harm to us hens, but with proper care and attention, you can keep them at bay. A clean, well-maintained coop is key to a healthy and happy flock. Let's dive into the details:

The Importance of Coop Cleanliness

A clean coop is essential to prevent pests and diseases. We hens prefer a tidy space, and when our environment is kept spick-and-span, we stay healthier and more productive. Here's how to maintain an im-peck-able coop:

Bedding Material: Line permanent floors with newspaper, wood chips, or sawdust for easy cleanup. Replace bedding weekly to remove droppings, prevent odors, and eliminate breeding grounds for harmful organisms.

Dropping Management: Scoop droppings daily, and add them to your compost pile or use them as fertilizer under shrubs. Chicken droppings are rich in nutrients that benefit your garden!

Removable Trays: Invest in a hen house design with removable trays under roosting areas and nest boxes for quick and efficient cleaning.

Monthly Deep Clean:

On a sunny day, let us fly the coop while you deep-clean the house. Use a water blaster or hose to scrub every nook and cranny, paying special attention to crevices where pests might hide.

Allow the coop to dry thoroughly before adding fresh straw or bedding. We go wild at the sight of fresh bedding, so be prepared for excited fluffing and ruffling when we return!

Common Pests and How to Prevent Them

Flies and Rodents: Decaying food scraps and soiled bedding can attract flies and rodents, which contaminate food and water and spread diseases. To prevent this:

- Remove uneaten scraps and spilled feed daily.

- Use hanging feeders and water dispensers, positioned at our head height to keep contents clean and out of reach of pests.

- Seal gaps or holes in the coop to block rodent entry.

Mites and Lice:

Mites and lice are external parasites that live under our feathers, causing itching, feather loss, and anemia from blood loss. The most common culprits include:

Northern Fowl Mites: Found around our vent area, causing irritation.

Red Mites: Hide in wood crevices during the day and feed on us at night as we sleep on the perch.

Scaly Leg Mites: Burrow under leg scales, causing swelling and discomfort.

Prevention Tips:

- Regularly inspect our feathers, vent area, and legs for signs of parasites.

- Spray coop surfaces with a natural disinfectant like a mix of water and apple cider vinegar to deter pests.

- Add diatomaceous earth to bedding and dust-bath areas to kill mites and lice naturally.

Dust Baths:

We love to take dust baths, as it helps us keep our feathers clean and free of pests. Provide a dust-bathing area filled with loose dirt, sand, and a sprinkling of wood ash or diatomaccous earth. It's like a spa day for us hens!

Predator Prevention

Rodents: Rodents not only steal our food but also raid nest boxes and contaminate the coop with their droppings. Ensure:

- All gaps in the coop are sealed with mesh or boards.

- Feeders and waterers are inaccessible to scavengers.

Aerial Predators: Hawks are a real threat, especially when we're free-ranging. Roosters are great at alerting us to danger, but you can also provide:

- Sheltered areas or shrubs where we can hide.

- Overhead netting in open runs to deter birds of prey.

Even seagulls flying overhead can send us squawking for cover, mistaking them for hawks!

Neighborhood Cats: Curious cats often wander into the yard to check us out. While larger hens can usually handle themselves, Bantams are more vulnerable. To keep us safe:

- Consider adding a small, energetic dog to the yard to deter feline visitors.

- Roosters are also excellent guardians and will chase away intruders.

Monitoring and Routine Maintenance

Daily Checks: Spend time observing us—our quirks and habits. If one of us seems lethargic or unusually quiet, it may be a sign of illness or stress.

Airflow and Ventilation: Ensure the coop has proper ventilation to prevent dampness and ammonia buildup. Stale air can cause respiratory problems and create an inviting environment for pests.

Summary of what We have Learned so Far

To simplify the matter from the start: if you have a clean coop, you can avoid many health problems. We girls like to be clean. To keep your chicken coop clean, you should: line permanent house floors with newspaper, natural wood chips, or sawdust so that it can be easily removed when cleaned out weekly.

Coop cleanliness is a sure-as-*eggs* way to promote good health in your backyard flock. Spending a little time, scoop in hand, removing droppings is a wonderful way to prevent illness. Recycle those collected droppings into the compost or under your shrubs. Soiled bedding is a breeding ground for harmful organisms. The henhouse design ideally should have removable trays, positioned under the nest boxes and under the roosting area, which makes the cleaning process even easier.

Maybe once a month, on a fine day, let the girls *fly the coop* and turn the water blaster on the house interior. This also allows you to get a *bird's* eye view inspection of crevices where undesirables can hide. Once dry, replace the bedding: we birds of a feather flock together and go crazy at the sight of fresh straw in the house.

Make sure the hen house is clean and im-*peck*-able, so you can prevent the following pest invasions:

Flies and Mice: Excess kai and bedding waste can attract flies and mice to a property. Not only do you have a pest problem, but their droppings can contaminate chicken feed and water.

So never allow scraps to remain on the ground, to go off, attracting the wrong kind of attention. An innovative idea is to place the feeder and water dispenser at the bird's height: this will keep the food and water clean and prevent wastage.

Apple Cider Vinegar is a wonderful natural cleaner for the entire chicken coop. Just mix a few teaspoons of this tonic with water in a spray bottle: spray surfaces including crevices; empty nest boxes; and perches; and wipe off. Routine use will help to disinfect and inhibit dust mites, mold, and odors from forming in your coop.

Lice, and three diverse types of mites: northern, scaly leg, and red, can live under the feathers and suck the blood, and diminish egg production. This problem can certainly *tick us off*. *Comb* the area for signs of pests before they become invasions.

Besides foraging, we will spend a good hour fluffing around in a soil crater, shaking all that dust through our feathers and then preening ourselves. If you provide us with such a 'bathing/beauty' area, you will be helping us rid ourselves of any possible external parasites.

It's quite a *peck*-culiar circumstance to watch hens squawk and dive under cover when a hawk is circling above in the sky. If free-ranging, nothing beats the watchful eyes of a rooster, whose duty it is to serve and protect. Oftentimes, a flying seagull is mistaken for a hawk and our instinct is to hide under cover.

Neighborhood cats visiting your property can also cause a flight response from us. In my opinion, often a cat is inquisitive as to what we are: being larger than the ordinary native birds. Free-ranging Bantams ought to be wary, but larger breeds should be okay.

<u>Thistle's Cleanliness Mantra:</u> "A clean coop keeps pests at bay, and a happy hen lays every day!"

I hope my advice helps you keep your flock pest-free and thriving. With regular cleaning, observation, and proactive pest control measures, you'll create a safe and comfortable home for us.

Now, if you'll excuse me, I have a date with a dust bath! – Thistle out!

About Common Ailments by Dropsy

Hello, flock fans! I'm Dropsy, and I'm here to share what I know about keeping your hens happy, healthy, and thriving. A little knowledge goes a long way in recognizing and managing common chicken ailments. By taking proactive steps, you can prevent many issues before they become serious.

Let's dive into some of the health challenges we hens might face and how you can help.

Ascites (Dropsy)

Healthy chooks equals happy chooks! You'll get out of your chickens what you put into them – literally. Take it from me, Dropsy! As my name suggests I have a health condition that affects my abdomen. Ascites (commonly called dropsy) is a condition that causes fluid buildup in the abdominal cavity, leading to a wide-legged stance that might be confused with an egg-bound hen.

Symptoms: Distended, fluid-filled abdomen, lethargy, and difficulty moving.

Causes: Internal laying, obesity, genetic predisposition, heart disease, or exposure to moldy feed or fungi.

Treatment: Unfortunately, dropsy is incurable. My condition is not common and only affects old girls like me. Dropsy is not contagious.

Consult with a vet to make your old bird more comfortable until her last sunset.

Prevention Tip: Ensure proper ventilation in the coop to reduce exposure to harmful molds and fungi. A coop with good airflow, free of drafts, promotes fresh air circulation and helps prevent respiratory and systemic diseases.

Botulism

Botulism is a serious condition caused by toxins from decaying organic matter, such as spoiled food or rotting carcasses.

Symptoms: Tremors, difficulty breathing, paralysis, and death if untreated.

Treatment: If caught early, mix 1 teaspoon of Epsom salts with 1 ounce of warm water and administer with a dropper into the hen's beak once daily.

Prevention Tip: Maintain coop cleanliness by ensuring feed is fresh, water is clean, and scraps are removed daily. Never leave raw or spoiled meat in the environment.

Bumblefoot

Bumblefoot is a bacterial infection in the sole of a hen's foot, usually caused by a cut or puncture wound from sharp objects in the yard.

Symptoms: Limping and a black, hardened cyst on the sole of the foot.

Treatment: Soak the affected foot in warm water mixed with Epsom salts to soften the skin.

Use tweezers to gently remove the hardened bumble.

Sanitize the area and wrap the foot with vet wrap to protect it as it heals.

Prevention Tip: Regularly inspect the yard for sharp objects and provide soft, clean bedding in the coop.

Fowl Pox

Fowl pox is a viral infection that causes unsightly lesions on a hen's face, comb, wattles, and legs.

Symptoms: Raised yellowish blisters that darken and scab over before falling off after about three weeks. Respiratory symptoms may include coughing and wheezing in severe cases.

Treatment: Dab the lesions with iodine to prevent secondary infections. For respiratory complications, consult a vet about antibiotics.

Prevention Tip: Reduce stress in your flock and support their immune systems with proper nutrition and a clean environment.

Sour Crop

Sour crop occurs when food remains in a hen's crop too long, leading to fermentation and bacterial growth.

Diet is the cause of this ailment such as: consuming strands of long stalky grass or bulky scraps.

Symptoms: A swollen, squishy crop, gurgling noises, and a yeasty smell from the hen's breath.

Treatment: You can check her out yourself: in the morning, feel her crop for fullness. Can you hear gurgling noises coming from her chest? Does her breath smell yeasty? If so, she will need to be isolated and go on a food fast for twelve hours. Massage her crop every couple of hours. Make sure she has access to clean water.

The following day, if the crop is flat then feed her small mushy meals (mash and scrambled egg) that are easily processed.

Prevention Tip: Avoid giving hens long, fibrous grasses or bulky scraps that may clog their crops.

Infectious Bronchitis

Infectious bronchitis is a highly contagious viral disease that affects the respiratory system. The production of eggs can drop dramatically... I mean, who wants to work while sick, right?

Symptoms: Coughing, sneezing, watery eyes, bubbling sounds when breathing, and a dramatic drop in egg production.

Treatment: While there is no cure, you can support recovery with protein-rich foods, vitamins, and plenty of fresh air.

Prevention Tip: Quarantine new birds before introducing them to your flock and maintain excellent biosecurity practices to prevent outbreaks.

Mycoplasma

Mycoplasma (Chronic Respiratory Disease) is a bacterial infection that weakens the immune system and spreads rapidly among hens. Other names for this disorder are Roop and Bulgy Eye.

Symptoms: Nasal discharge, coughing, fatigue, loss of appetite, gaping, and a foul smell around the head.

Treatment: Quarantine affected hens and consult a vet for antibiotics.

Prevention Tip: Incorporate natural herbs like thyme, oregano, lemon balm, and garlic into the flock's diet to strengthen their immune systems. Add apple cider vinegar or colloidal silver to drinking water monthly for added protection.

Proactive Steps for a Healthy Flock

Daily Observation: Spend time with your hens to learn their personalities and notice any changes in behavior. A hen that isolates herself, appears lethargic, or moves differently may need closer examination.

Cleanliness and Ventilation: Keep the coop clean and dry to reduce the risk of disease.

Ensure adequate ventilation to prevent dampness and ammonia buildup. Install vents on one side of the coop, away from prevailing winds, to promote fresh airflow.

The house design should enable fresh air movement but exclude any draught in cooler weather. Fresh air pushes out stale air and excess moisture. Dampness and ammonia build-up are a sign that there is not enough ventilation. Regular humid conditions can cause health problems in your flock to emerge. Vents on one side of the house will usually give plenty of ventilation. Check where your prevailing winds come from and position the house in such a way that the ladies aren't blown away.

Nutritious Diet: Feed your flock a balanced diet of high-quality layer feed, supplemented with fresh greens, protein sources, and occasional herbs. Avoid moldy feed, which can lead to serious health issues.

Supplements and Immune Boosters: Add apple cider vinegar (1 tablespoon per 2 liters) to water to improve digestion and reduce harmful bacteria.

Include calcium supplements, like oyster shells or dried, crushed eggshells, to support eggshell quality.

Rotate a natural herb tincture in drinking water monthly to prevent respiratory infections.

Vaccinations: Consider vaccinating your flock against common diseases like fowl pox and infectious bronchitis to minimize outbreaks.

Final Thoughts: Caring for Your Flock

Healthy chooks truly equal happy chooks! With proper care, nutrition, and cleanliness, your hens will reward you with their best: delicious eggs and lively companionship.

Hanging out with your feathered friends is good for their wellbeing. The ladies get to know you and you get to know them: their individual personalities and quirks, as some hens will be serious and quiet, while others will be boisterous and mischievous.

By observing your flock, you can pick up tell-tale signs that a hen is unwell due to how she interacts with others and moves about. If you notice that a hen is off to one side, looking lethargic or quieter than her usual self, you'd best take a closer look.

As Johan always says, "A well-tended flock is a *feather* in your cap." Now, if you'll excuse me, I'm off for a health *chick*! Dropsy out!

About Handling Hens by Dandelion

Hello there! I'm Dandelion, here to tell you how to strengthen your bond with your chickens and make the most of your time together. A little daily interaction goes a long way in building trust, which makes caring for us easier and more enjoyable for everyone involved.

Daily Interaction: Building Trust

As you go about your yard chores or enjoy a morning coffee, take a moment to chat with us hens. We're great listeners! By spending time with us every day, you'll:

Strengthen Recognition: With consistent interaction, we'll learn to recognize your voice and face. Over time, we'll associate you with safety and treats, which helps during inspections or when one of us needs to be caught.

Encourage Trust: When we trust you, we're easier to manage—whether you're clipping wings, checking for health issues, or moving us to a new location.

Tips for Engagement:

Turn Over Stones or Logs: Reveal tasty bugs and watch us scramble in delight—it's like opening a treasure chest for us!

Hand-Feed Treats: Offer grains, apple slices, or greens from your hand. This not only helps us associate you with positive experiences but also teaches us to come when called.

Chat While Strolling: Talk to us as you wander the yard. Even if you're discussing the weather, we'll cluck back in agreement.

Managing Flighty Hens

Most of us hens can only manage short flights—enough to get over a hedge or fence. To keep us safely contained, it's a good idea to clip one wing's flight feathers.

How to Clip Flight Feathers:

Frequency: Clipping is usually needed 1–2 times per year, typically after we moult.

Method: Research the proper technique first—don't wing it!

- Use sharp scissors to carefully trim the primary feathers on one wing.

- Work in a dimly lit room, which calms us, and speak softly to reassure us.

- Always have a helper to hold us securely but gently.

Other Clipping Needs:

Toenails: If we're not free-ranging often, our nails can grow too long and require trimming.

Beaks: Occasionally, a beak tip may overgrow and need a gentle trim. Again, research or consult an expert before attempting.

Free-Range Fun (With Boundaries!)

Allowing us to free-range is wonderful for our health and happiness, but it comes with responsibilities. While we love scratching, foraging, and exploring, we might wander into places we shouldn't—like your flowerbeds!

Tips for Free-Range Success:

Mobile Fencing: Use a portable fence to restrict us to certain areas. This way, we can help prepare your garden soil or munch on pests without wreaking havoc.

Provide a Dust Bath Area: Fresh soil or sand is irresistible to us. We love to create hollows for dust baths, which keep us clean by removing oil and mites from our feathers. Johan had the great idea of using a 60x40cm plastic bin filled with dirt inside the coop for a designated dust bath area. Genius, right?

Evening Check-Ins: If we're free-ranging during the day, count us as we return to roost in the evening. This ensures everyone is safe, sound, and accounted for.

What do chicken families do on Saturday afternoons? They go on peck-nics!

Healthy Behaviors and Signs of Wellness

Healthy hens are active, curious, and social. We'll spend our days:

Pecking and Scratching: Exploring the ground for bugs, seeds, and tasty morsels.

<u>Preening:</u> Keeping our feathers clean and shiny.

<u>Gossiping:</u> Yes, we chat! If you listen closely, you'll notice different clucks and sounds for various moods and activities.

<u>Key Signs of Health:</u>

- Bright red combs and wattles.

- Clear, shiny eyes.

- Clean feathers, especially around the vent area.

If one of us seems lethargic, isolates herself, or stops eating, it's time to take a closer look. Early intervention can prevent minor issues from becoming major problems.

Enrichment and Boredom Busters

We're clever birds and need mental stimulation to stay happy. A good keeper imagines ways to keep us entertained, especially during confinement.

<u>Ideas for Enrichment:</u>

<u>Hanging Treats:</u> Tie up leafy greens or vegetable scraps at various heights for us to peck at. It's fun and keeps us active.

<u>Ramps and Perches:</u> Add different levels in the coop for climbing and roosting.

<u>Interactive Toys:</u> Scatter food puzzles or rolling treat dispensers in the run to challenge our foraging skills.

Daily and Weekly Care Routines

Caring for your hens doesn't require much time, but regular routines ensure a happy, healthy flock:

Daily Tasks:

- Supply fresh food and water.
- Collect eggs in the evening.
- Check that the coop is clean and secure.

Weekly Tasks:

- Replace soiled bedding in the nest boxes.
- Disinfect feeders, waterers, and surfaces.
- Inspect the flock for signs of illness or injury.

The Rewards of Keeping Chickens

After the initial setup, keeping hens is one of the most rewarding and sustainable ways to enrich your life. They provide:

Sustainable Living: Hens recycle kitchen scraps, fertilize your garden, and reduce waste.

Cost Savings: Fewer trips to buy eggs, plus the joy of eating fresh, high-quality ones.

Endless Entertainment: Chickens have unique personalities—some are boisterous, others gentle. Spending time with us is always a treat!

What's a chicken's favorite movie genre? A chick flick!

Final Thoughts: Feathered Companions for Life

Keeping chickens isn't just about the eggs; it's about the bond you form with your flock. With just a little effort, you'll create a safe, stimulating environment where we can thrive. We'll reward you with our quirky antics, natural pest control, and, of course, delicious eggs.

As you go about your yard chores or take a stroll, engage with your feathered friends: chat with us; pat us. Roll over a stone or log to show us tasty critters. Chat with us over your morning coffee. With a healthy amount of bonding your chickens will recognize your voice and face. This means that trust is built up to manage the hens when inspections are required or when trying to coral a hen who has flown the coop.

Hens are a tremendous help in the garden. We will weed soil for you by scratching through it and eating pests like snails and aphids. If you have a mobile fence, you can use it to contain us in an area that you want worked over.

A good hen keeper will imagine ways to stave off boredom for his ladies: green vegetable leaves can be hung up in various places, so we birds can peck at them; ramps and various levels within the coop, are all great ideas for behavioral enrichment of your chickens.

Caring for your hens does not take long. Twice daily, supply fresh food and water, collect any eggs, check the coop is sanitary, and troubleshoot any problems. Once a week, change the nest material and disinfect the coop.

After the initial start-up costs, keeping chickens is one of the most affordable and rewarding pets on offer. For any animal lover, keeping chickens is a rewarding experience that you can savor for many years. You will always remember your feathered friends.

Keeping chooks is a satisfying way to live more sustainably and help the environment: hens eliminate scraps, produce an effective fertilizer for the garden, and remember the cost saving on all those eggs! Keeping chickens is a way to start living green.

Now, if you'll excuse me, I'm off to watch a chick flick with the girls. Keep cluckin'! – Dandelion

PART TWO
THOSE BORN IN POULTSVILLE

About Roosters by Perky

Gidday! My name is Perky, and I'm here to crow about what it means to be a rooster. While I may not lay eggs, I more than make up for it with my striking appearance, protective nature, and tireless devotion to my ladies. Let me take you through the ins and outs of rooster life, from my dawn wake-up calls to my duties as flock protector and, of course, my romantic escapades.

How to Spot a Rooster

You can tell I'm a rooster at a glance. I stand out from the ladies with:

Striking Plumage: My feathers are often more vibrant and glossy, with bold colors that make me the showstopper of the yard.

Long Tail Feathers: These elegant, flowing feathers add to my grandeur.

Larger Comb and Wattles: The bright red comb on my head and wattles under my beak are larger and more pronounced compared to hens.

No Egg-Laying Abilities: Yep, no eggs from me—just lots of crowing and charisma!

The Alarm Cluck: Crowing at Dawn

What am I most famous for? My crowing, of course! At the break of dawn, I belt out my signature tune to let everyone know it's a new day. My crowing doesn't stop there—it's how I mark my territory and assert my dominance.

What do you call a rooster who wakes you up every morning?

An alarm cluck!

I don't mean to disturb your shuteye; I crow because I feel an instinctive need to announce my presence and keep my flock safe. Crowing is my way of saying, "This is my yard, my ladies, and my watch."

Flock Protector: My Most Important Role

As a rooster, my prime duty is to protect my flock. My testosterone-fueled instincts make me ever vigilant, always scanning for threats and defending my territory. Whether it's a hawk overhead, the neighbor's cat, or an unexpected visitor, I'll step up without hesitation to confront the intruder.

How I Protect My Flock:

Predator Alerts: If I spot danger, I sound a series of low clucks to warn my ladies to stay close and be vigilant. If the threat gets too close, my clucking turns to a sharp alarm to scatter the flock into hiding.

Aggressive Defense: Should a predator or intruder come near, I puff up my feathers, charge forward, and let them know they've crossed the line. Trust me, there's no such thing as a chicken-livered rooster!

Should You Get a Rooster?

Before you rush to add a rooster to your backyard, here are a few things to consider:

Noise Levels: My crowing isn't limited to dawn—I'll sound off throughout the day. Some town councils prohibit roosters in residential areas, so check local bylaws before bringing me home.

Behavior Management: I'm naturally territorial, and while I can become friendly with regular interaction, my hormones might make me defensive. Adults can manage me, but children should always be supervised.

Training Tips:

- Spend time with me daily, offering treats and talking softly to earn my trust.

- Never show fear—stand your ground and gently assert your presence in the flock. If I trust you, I might even reward you with a little rooster dance!

Free-Ranging with a Rooster

If your flock is free-ranging, I'm your best investment for keeping the girls safe. My keeper, Johan, learned this firsthand. Without a rooster, the hens would heckle Johan to step in as their protector. But with me around, they can focus on foraging while I keep a watchful eye.

Common Threats I Defend Against:

Hawks: When a hawk circles overhead, I warn the flock and lead them to safety.

Cats and Dogs: Curious cats or neighbor dogs don't scare me. I'll confront them head-on if they invade our space.

Roosters and the Pecking Order

In any flock, there's a pecking order—a hierarchy that determines who's boss. My presence can actually reduce squabbling among the hens by providing a strong central figure to maintain order.

Multiple Roosters:

It's possible to have more than one rooster in a flock, but success depends on:

Space: The coop and run must be spacious enough to prevent territorial disputes.

Age: Roosters of similar age often get along better, as they grow up establishing their roles together.

Expanding Your Flock: The Natural Way

Want to grow your flock the old-fashioned way? That's where I shine! With me around, any broody hen sitting on fertilized eggs can hatch chicks, giving you control over your flock's future.

Hatching the Next Generation:

My reproductive fluids remain viable inside a hen for up to two weeks, meaning I don't need to mate daily to keep the eggs fertilized.

Once chicks hatch, they'll include a mix of pullets (future egg-layers) and cockerels (future roosters).

Courting the Ladies

Roosters are true gentlemen when it comes to courting. I don't just mate indiscriminately—I woo my ladies with charm and respect.

Courtship Rituals:

Food Offering: I scratch the ground and cluck softly to point out food to my hens, letting them eat first.

Dancing: I puff up my vibrant plumage, dip my wings, and perform a dance to impress a hen.

Mating: If she accepts my advances, I mate with her, and the cycle of life continues.

Why Looks Matter: Hens are drawn to roosters with large, bright red combs, long spurs, and glossy feathers. My flamboyant appearance signals my health and vitality, making me the ideal partner.

Fun Crack: I started a chicken dating website. It's not my full-time job; I just do it to make h*ens* meet!

Roosters: The Complete Package

Whether you're looking to protect a free-ranging flock, expand your flock naturally, or simply add a dash of flair to your backyard, a rooster can be a valuable and rewarding addition.

Key Takeaways:

- I'm territorial but trainable—bond with me, and I'll see you as a friend, not a threat.

- I'm always on guard, ensuring my ladies are safe from predators.

- With me around, you can enjoy the beauty of nature's cycle, from fertilized eggs to fluffy chicks.

Rooster Care and Integrating a Rooster into Your Flock

Roosters are an asset to many backyard flocks, offering protection, social stability, and natural flock expansion. But bringing a rooster into your flock requires preparation and ongoing care to ensure harmony and health. Let's dive into the details of rooster care and successful integration.

Rooster Care Essentials

Diet and Nutrition

Roosters have similar dietary needs to hens but require slightly less calcium since they don't lay eggs. Here's what a balanced diet for a rooster looks like:

Layer Feed: Fine for roosters if they share the coop with hens. If kept separately, you can use an all-flock feed, which provides balanced nutrition without excess calcium.

Protein-Rich Treats: Offer mealworms, sunflower seeds, or scrambled eggs occasionally to support muscle and feather health.

Greens and Veggies: Leafy greens, fruits, and vegetable scraps add variety and essential nutrients to his diet.

Grit and Oyster Shells: Ensure access to grit for digestion and oyster shells for any calcium needs (particularly if sharing feed with hens).

Tip: Always provide fresh, clean water, especially in hot weather when dehydration can affect a rooster's ability to perform his protective duties.

Health Maintenance

Roosters are hardy creatures but still require regular health checks:

Inspect Comb and Wattles: Should be bright red, smooth, and free of lesions or frostbite in colder months.

Check Feet and Spurs: Spurs grow continuously and may require trimming if they become overly long or sharp. A vet or experienced keeper can show you how to file them safely.

Feathers: Look for signs of mites, lice, or excessive wear from scuffles or mating. Regular dust baths help prevent external parasites.

Behavioral Monitoring: A sudden change in behavior (e.g., lethargy or aggression) could indicate illness or stress.

Managing Behavior

Roosters are driven by hormones, which can sometimes lead to aggressive or territorial behavior. To manage this:

Spend Time with Him Daily: Bond with your rooster through regular interaction. Talk softly and handle him gently when needed.

Assert Your Role: If he tests boundaries, stand your ground confidently. Avoid showing fear or retreating, as this may reinforce his dominance.

Limit Aggression: If a rooster becomes overly aggressive, use calming techniques such as carrying him briefly to assert control or distracting him with food or treats.

Supervision with Children and Pets: Roosters can become protective around unfamiliar individuals, especially small children. Always supervise interactions to prevent accidental scratches or pecks.

What do you call a chicken that crosses the road?

Poultry in motion.

Integrating a Rooster into Your Flock

Adding a rooster to an existing flock requires careful planning to minimize disruption and ensure a smooth transition.

Step 1: Assess Your Flock's Needs

Flock Size: A good ratio is one rooster for every 8-10 hens to prevent over-mating. Too few hens may lead to stress and feather damage from excessive attention.

Space: Roosters require adequate room to establish their territory and avoid unnecessary conflicts. Each bird should have at least 4 square feet of coop space and 10 square feet of run space.

Step 2: Choose the Right Rooster

If you're adding a new rooster, consider these factors:

Age: A young cockerel (less than a year old) is more likely to integrate smoothly than an older, dominant rooster.

Temperament: Choose a calm, docile breed like an Orpington or Brahma if your flock is timid. More assertive breeds, like Rhode Island Reds, may work better with confident hens.

Step 3: Quarantine the New Rooster

Before introducing the rooster to the flock:

Isolate for 2–4 Weeks: Place the rooster in a separate enclosure to monitor for signs of illness (e.g., coughing, sneezing, or mites).

Establish Familiarity: Position the quarantine area close enough for the flock to see and hear the rooster without direct contact. This helps everyone get used to each other's presence.

Step 4: Slow Introduction

Initial Interaction: After the quarantine period, allow the rooster and hens to interact through a barrier, such as wire fencing, for a few days. This prevents direct aggression while allowing the flock to establish a social hierarchy.

Supervised Free-Ranging: Let the rooster and hens forage together in a neutral area where territorial instincts are less pronounced.

Step 5: Monitor Pecking Order Dynamics

Once the rooster is fully integrated into the coop:

Observe Behavior: Some squabbling is normal as the flock adjusts, but intervene if there's persistent aggression or injury.

Support Lower-Ranking Hens: Ensure timid hens have access to food, water, and safe spaces if they're being chased or bullied.

Rooster Roles in the Flock

Guardian: Roosters are natural protectors, always scanning for predators and sounding alarms to warn the hens. They'll lead the flock to safety if danger is near.

Mediator: Roosters help maintain order by reducing hen-on-hen squabbles.

Courting and Mating: A rooster ensures flock continuity by fertilizing eggs for broody hens to hatch.

Benefits of Keeping a Rooster

Protection: Roosters are your flock's first line of defense against predators.

Flock Stability: They establish a hierarchy, reducing hen conflicts.

Natural Breeding: A rooster enables you to expand your flock the natural way, without purchasing new chicks.

Flock Bonding: Watching a rooster lead, dance for, and care for his hens is one of the joys of chicken keeping.

Final Thoughts on Rooster Care

Roosters bring flair, functionality, and a touch of drama to your backyard flock. With proper care and thoughtful integration, they can be a valuable addition to your chicken-keeping experience. Whether they're defending the flock, charming the ladies, or serenading the sunrise, roosters add personality and purpose to your coop.

So, if you're ready to embrace a feathered guardian, don't *wing* it—plan ahead, show patience, and enjoy the unique rewards of rooster ownership.

Now, if you'll excuse me, I have a dance to rehearse for the ladies. Crow you later! – Perky.

About Hatching Chickens by Freckle

What did one hatching chick say to the other hatching chick?

The last one out is a rotten egg.

When it comes to jokes, I'm the king of the roost. My name is Freckle and I'm going to *egg* you on to hatch your own cute chickens.

There truly is an art to hatching your own eggs or raising day-old chicks that you have bought. Starting your own flock from scratch is a very interesting hobby. It is time to *spread your wings* and try something new.

Hatching your own chickens is one of the most rewarding experiences you can have as a poultry keeper. Whether you're using a broody hen or an artificial incubator, the process is filled with anticipation, wonder, and, let's admit it—an endless supply of chicken jokes. So, let's crack into it!

Broody Hens: Nature's Incubator

If you have a broody hen, congratulations! You've got the easiest and most natural path to hatching chicks. A broody hen will do all the hard work for you, from keeping the eggs warm and humid to teaching the chicks how to peck and forage after they hatch.

Signs of a Broody Hen:

- She spends all day in the nest, fluffed up and clucking softly.
- She pecks or squawks when disturbed, fiercely defending her eggs.
- She stops laying eggs to focus on incubation.

Setting the Eggs:

Number of Eggs: A medium-to-large hen can incubate up to five eggs comfortably.

Egg Timing: Ensure the eggs are of a similar age so the chicks develop and hatch simultaneously.

Nighttime Placement: If you choose to introduce eggs to her nest, do it at night, as broody hens are calmer and less likely to be disturbed.

The Broody Hen's Role:

Once the eggs are in place, the hen takes over, maintaining the ideal temperature and turning the eggs regularly. She rarely leaves the nest, so place feed and water nearby to ensure she stays nourished.

Hatching Day: Around day 21, the hen will hear soft peeping from inside the eggs. She'll respond with gentle clucks to encourage the chicks to break through their shells.

It may take up to two days for all the chicks to hatch, during which the hen will stay on the nest. Afterward, she'll lead her new brood out of the nest and teach them how to eat, drink, and scratch.

Why couldn't the hen find her eggs?

Because she mis*laid* them.

Helpful Tips:

- Have a brooder setup ready in case the hen abandons the nest before all the eggs have hatched.

- Avoid disturbing the hen and chicks during the hatching process—it's a delicate time for them.

Artificial Incubators: Hatching Without a Hen

If you don't have a broody hen or want to hatch a larger number of chicks, an artificial incubator is your next best option.

Choosing an Incubator:

Manual Incubators: These are affordable but require you to turn the eggs by hand multiple times daily.

Automatic Incubators: Pricier, but have conveniences like automatic egg turners, temperature control, and humidity management.

Forced Air Incubators: Equipped with fans to circulate air evenly for consistent temperature and humidity.

The Egg Incubation Process:

Buy Fertilized Eggs: Source eggs from a reputable breeder. Ensure the eggs are clean but not washed, as washing removes the protective bloom that shields them from bacteria.

Temperature: Maintain a constant 37–38°C (99–100°F) throughout the incubation process.

Humidity:

Days 1–18: 58–60%.

Days 19–21: Increase to 65%.

Turning the Eggs: Mark an X and O on opposite sides of each egg and turn them at least three times daily until day 18. Automatic incubators handle this for you.

Hatching Time: On day 21, chicks will start to pip (crack the shell). It may take several hours for them to fully emerge, so resist the urge to intervene unless absolutely necessary.

Ventilation: Open the incubator's air vents gradually as hatching begins to ensure proper oxygen flow.

Caring for New Hatchlings

Once the chicks have hatched, they'll need warmth, food, and water to thrive.

Brooder Setup: A brooder is a safe, enclosed area where chicks can grow during their first few weeks.

Heat Source: Provide a heat lamp or heating plate to maintain a temperature of 32–35°C (90–95°F) during the first week, gradually reducing by 2.5°C (5°F) each week.

Bedding: Line the brooder with newspaper covered by soft wood shavings or paper towels to prevent splayed legs. Avoid slippery surfaces like smooth cardboard.

Feed and Water: Provide chick starter feed, which is high in protein to support rapid growth, and a shallow water dish to prevent drowning.

Monitor Chicks Closely:

Healthy chicks will be active, chirping, and exploring their surroundings.

Keep an eye on their temperature needs—if they huddle under the heat source, they're too cold; if they scatter to the edges, it's too warm.

What do you do with a shy chick?

Try to get it to come out of its shell.

Discarding Unhatched Eggs

By day 26, any remaining unhatched eggs should be discarded, as they are unlikely to hatch and could become a source of bacteria.

Expanding Your Flock Naturally

One of the benefits of hatching your own chicks is that it allows you to grow your flock sustainably:

Broody Hens as Teachers: Once the chicks are hatched, the mother hen will integrate them into the flock, teaching them social skills and how to forage.

Sexing Chicks: After a few weeks, you'll be able to identify which chicks are cockerels (young roosters) and which are pullets (young hens). Plan accordingly for space, as too many roosters can lead to conflicts.

I had a hen who could count her own eggs. She was a *mathamachicken.*

Tips for Success in Backyard Hatching

Be Patient: Hatching is a slow process, especially on day 21. Trust nature and resist the urge to intervene unless absolutely necessary.

Practice Good Hygiene: Wash your hands before handling eggs and keep the incubator clean to prevent contamination.

Get the Kids Involved: Hatching chicks is an excellent educational experience for children, teaching them about biology, responsibility, and the miracle of life.

What happens if someone cracks an egg on your head?

The yolk's on you.

Final Thoughts from Freckle

Hatching chicks is an exciting way to start or expand your flock. Whether you rely on the steady dedication of a broody hen or the precise control of an incubator, the process is sure to be egg-citing!

Remember, patience and preparation are key to success. So go ahead, spread your wings, and give hatching a go!

What do you call someone who knows everything about hatching chicks?

An egg-spert!

How do you know if these egg jokes are good?

If they crack you up.

Well, that's all from me. Time to crack some more yolks with my flock. See you around the yard! – Freckle

About Raising Chicks by Lanky Doodle

Raising Chickens: From Fluffy Cheeps to Backyard Beauties with a cluck from Lanky Doodle!

Why did the chicken cross the basketball court? Because the referee cried fowl! Jokes aside, raising chickens is a rewarding and educational experience that brings joy and sustainability to your backyard. Whether you're starting with a broody hen or an incubator, this guide will help you nurture those cheeping fluff balls into healthy, happy hens and cockerels.

Getting Started: Brooder Setup for Chicks

Timing and Transition

If you're using a broody hen, she'll handle the hard work, from keeping her chicks warm to teaching them how to peck and forage. But for incubator-hatched chicks, it's your turn to step in!

Allow the chicks 24 hours to dry and fluff up inside the incubator before moving them.

Newly hatched chicks don't need food or water immediately; their yolk sac provides nutrition for the first 48 hours.

Setting Up the Brooder

A brooder is a safe, draft-free environment where chicks can grow during their first few weeks. Here's how to create the perfect space:

Box Size: Use a large, sturdy box or container that gives each chick at least 0.5 square feet of space, increasing as they grow.

Bedding: For the first week, line the brooder floor with paper towels to prevent the chicks from eating litter. Afterward, transition to soft pine shavings (not cedar) or straw. Avoid sawdust, as chicks might ingest it.

Heat Source: Use a heat lamp or heating plate to maintain a temperature of 32–35°C (90–95°F) during the first week.

Gradually lower the temperature by 2.5°C (5°F) each week until the chicks are fully feathered at about 6–8 weeks old.

Place the heat source on one side of the brooder, allowing chicks to move closer or further away to regulate their comfort.

Tip: Watch the chicks' behavior to assess their temperature needs. If they huddle under the lamp, they're too cold. If they scatter to the edges, they're too warm.

Food and Water for Chicks

Feeding

- Start chicks on starter crumble, a high-protein feed formulated for their growth needs. It's readily available at rural supply stores.

- Serve food in shallow containers or trays to make it easy for chicks to find and access.

Treats: Small amounts of scrambled eggs are a fantastic treat, packed with nutrients. But avoid giving sugary or fatty scraps at this stage.

Watering

- Provide clean, fresh water in a shallow dish to prevent drowning. Consider a waterer designed for chicks, placed at wing height to keep it clean.

- Gently dip the beak of each chick into the water to show them where it is. They'll catch on quickly!

- Change water frequently to prevent contamination and bacterial growth.

Health and Hygiene: Keeping Chicks Happy

Raising chicks requires vigilance to ensure they stay healthy. Make sure your box is im-*peck*-ably clean. Cleanliness and monitoring are critical during these early weeks, as chicks are highly vulnerable to diseases.

Brooder Cleanliness

- Remove droppings and replace soiled bedding daily to maintain a sanitary environment.

- Never leave damp food in the brooder, as it can harbor fungi or bacteria harmful to chicks.

- Wash feed and water containers regularly to prevent buildup of mold or residue.

Common Chick Ailments and How to Prevent Them

Brooder Pneumonia (Aspergillosis):

Cause: Fungal infection from moldy bedding, damp feed, or poor ventilation.

Symptoms: Loss of appetite, respiratory gasping, lethargy, and sleepiness.

Prevention:

- Keep the brooder dry and well-ventilated.

- Regularly replace bedding and ensure feed is stored in a dry, cool place.

- Quarantine and seek veterinary advice for infected chicks.

Coccidiosis:

Cause: A parasitic infection spread through droppings, often exacerbated by overcrowding or poor hygiene.

Symptoms: Diarrhea, lethargy, loss of appetite, pale comb, and ruffled feathers.

Prevention:

- Use medicated starter crumble or vaccinate chicks to protect against coccidiosis.

- Clean the brooder frequently and provide adequate space and ventilation.

Important: Chicks gradually develop immunity to coccidiosis by about 8 weeks old, but severe cases can cause long-term health problems in survivors.

Behavior and Enrichment for Growing Chicks

Social Development

Chicks are naturally curious and social animals. By interacting with them regularly, you'll help them grow into confident, friendly birds.

Talk to Them: Sit near the brooder and softly talk to the chicks. They'll quickly learn to recognize your voice.

Hand Feeding: Gently offer small treats from your hand to build trust and encourage bonding.

Enrichment Ideas

Mini Perches: Add low perches to the brooder after a few weeks to encourage natural roosting behaviors.

Foraging Fun: Sprinkle a small amount of crumble or tiny treats on the brooder floor for chicks to "hunt" and scratch for.

Mirrors: Place a small, shatterproof mirror in the brooder. Chicks love to investigate their reflections!

Transitioning Chicks to the Outdoors

By 6–8 weeks, your chicks should be fully feathered and ready to move into their permanent coop.

Gradual Exposure:

Introduce chicks to the outdoors in a small, supervised enclosure during warm, sunny days to help them acclimate.

Return them to the brooder at night until temperatures are consistently above 16°C (60°F).

Integration with the Flock:

Introduce chicks to older birds gradually to minimize pecking order conflicts. Use a wire barrier to let them see and interact without direct contact for a few days.

Provide plenty of space, feeders, and waterers to reduce competition.

Coop Preparation:

Ensure the coop is clean, predator-proof, and equipped with roosts, nesting boxes, and proper ventilation.

Provide enough space—each chicken needs 4 square feet of coop space and 10 square feet of run space.

Raising Chickens: The Joys and Rewards

Raising chicks is more than just a backyard project—it's a fulfilling journey that teaches patience, responsibility, and the wonders of nature. Watching your fluffy cheep-cheeps grow into beautiful, productive chickens is a source of endless pride and enjoyment.

Benefits of Raising Chickens:

Educational for Kids: A hands-on way to learn about life cycles, animal care, and sustainability.

Fresh Eggs: By raising your own flock, you'll enjoy fresh, delicious eggs with the satisfaction of knowing exactly how your hens were raised.

Sustainable Living: Chickens recycle food scraps, fertilize your garden, and reduce your household's waste.

Final Words from Lanky Doodle:

Raising chicks is an adventure filled with laughs, learning, and lots of cheeping. Remember, a clean brooder, plenty of care, and lots of love will help your chicks thrive into adulthood.

Why is it easy for chicks to talk?

Because talk is *cheep.*

Cluck you later, folks! – Lanky Doodle.

Well, *wattle* you know, it's the end of my chapter and the book. And for completing the book, go ahead and place a *feather* in your cap.

From all of us HENS IN POULTSVILLE - thanks for taking us under your wing!

We hope one day all chickens will be free to cross the road without having their motives questioned.

Meet J Pilgrim

This renowned author has engaged readers worldwide with his published books on philosophy, wellness, and fiction. He has a portfolio of eBooks and printed works on all good online bookstores.

His works delve deep into the human spirit, exploring the profound questions that have intrigued thinkers for centuries. Through these writings, the author offers readers a chance to embark on their own journeys of self-discovery and enlightenment.

The author was raised on a farm and kept poultry. As a teenager, he gave names to the hens and roosters and captures them in this long-awaited book.

This fun and informative book on backyard poultry keeping is a must for any young person who wants to *spread their wings* into this amazing hobby.

Now older, the author has retained his love for his feathered friends and shares advice for any chicken enthusiast.

Available Worldwide

The author's eBooks and printed works are available at all good online bookstores, making it easy for readers across the globe to access his insightful and entertaining writings. Whether you're seeking profound philosophical insights, practical wellness advice, or an epic fantasy adventure, J Pilgrim has something to offer.

Connect with J Pilgrim

Stay updated on J Pilgrim's latest releases, and more by following him on Books2Read. Join a community of readers who are inspired, entertained, and transformed by the works of J Pilgrim.

www.thetrioniansaga.weebly.com

Also by J Pilgrim

The Trionian Saga

The Trionian Saga - Part One: Beyond the Border Mountains
The Trionian Saga - Part Two: The Hyna Sword
The Trionian Saga - Part Three: The Quest for Lyla

Standalone

The Hens in Poultsville
Sleeping with Crystal
Excel Your Wellness: Virtues and Vitamins
The Chi Key
Body Strengthening Strategy
Xcel Wellness Tai Chi

Watch for more at www.thetrioniansaga.weebly.com.

About the Publisher

From the PublisherThe author's eBooks and printed works are available at all good online bookstores, making it easy for readers across the globe to access his insightful and entertaining writings. Whether you're seeking profound philosophical insights, practical wellness advice, or an epic fantasy adventure, J Pilgrim has something to offer.Connect with J PilgrimStay updated on J Pilgrim's latest releases, and more by following him on Books2Read. Join a community of readers who are inspired, entertained, and transformed by the works of J Pilgrim.

Read more at www.thetrioniansaga.weebly.com.

www.ingramcontent.com/pod-product-compliance
Lightning Source LLC
LaVergne TN
LVHW040947150826
845672LV00002B/571

* 9 7 9 8 2 3 0 0 2 7 1 5 7 *